Ten Bedtim

Volume One

ex libris

Candlestick Press

Published by:
Candlestick Press,
Diversity House, 72 Nottingham Road,
Arnold, Nottingham NG5 6LF
www.candlestickpress.co.uk

Design, typesetting, print and production by Diversity Creative
Marketing Solutions Ltd., www.diversitymarketing.co.uk

Illustration © Judy Stevens, 2013 www.nbillustration.co.uk/judy-stevens
Introduction and selection © William Boyd, 2013

ISBN 978 1 907598 18 0

Acknowledgements:
Candlestick Press wishes to thank William Boyd for his generosity.
Thanks are also due to The Gallery Press for permission to reprint
'Champagne' by Medbh McGuckian from *The Flower Master* (Oxford
University Press, 1986) and 'Songs of Praise' by Derek Mahon from
Collected Poems (The Gallery Press, 1999). Excerpt from 'Out on the
lawn I lie in bed' by W. H. Auden is reprinted from *Selected Poems* (Faber
and Faber Ltd, 1979), Copyright © W H Auden. Reprinted by permission
of Curtis Brown Ltd. 'The Armadillo' by Elizabeth Bishop is from *The
Complete Poems 1927-1979* (Chatto and Windus, 1991). Copyright © 1979,
1983 Alice Helen Methfessel. Reprinted by permission of Farrar, Straus
and Giroux, LLC. 'Sad Steps' by Philip Larkin is reprinted from *Collected
Poems* (The Marvell Press and Faber and Faber Ltd, 1988); 'Preludes: 1'
by T. S. Eliot is reprinted from *Collected Poems 1909 – 1962*, (Faber and
Faber Ltd, 1963); 'Two Figures in Dense Violet Night' by Wallace Stevens
is reprinted from *Collected Poems*, (Faber and Faber Ltd, 2006); 'A Safe
Distance' by Jamie McKendrick is reprinted from *Out There* (Faber and
Faber Ltd, 2012). 'Evening' by Christopher Reid is from *Nonsense* (Faber
and Faber Ltd, 2012), Copyright © Christopher Reid 2012. Reproduced
by permission of the author c/o Rogers, Coleridge & White Ltd., 20 Powis
Mews, London W11 1JN. 'Heaven on Earth' by Craig Raine is reprinted
from *Clay. Whereabouts Unknown* (Penguin Books, 1996).

Introduction

I can't prove this assertion, but my own instinct, a certain amount of anecdotal evidence and the odd give-away remark by some of my contemporaries tell me that novelists – serious novelists, that is, literary novelists – read a lot of poetry. This is definitely true in my own case. The first writers I came to know personally were poets and I spent eight years failing to complete a PhD on another poet, Percy Bysshe Shelley. This may explain why I'm a compulsive reader and buyer of poetry but I think there's something deeper. Novelists go to poetry in a state of benign envy, I believe. It's the overt manipulation of language that attracts, the density of effect as well as sheer lyrical beauty. Novelists deal with these concepts as well, of course, but in a novel such rich language-use tends to be sporadic or necessarily diluted (unless you're writing *Finnegans Wake*). The freedom to exploit the full potency of the English language, to plunder and deform, surprise and astonish, juxtapose and allude is the freedom that only the poet possesses - and the novelist looks on marvelling and enthralled.

All this is by way of preamble to this choice of ten poems by ten poets. All these poets are favourites of mine and have a secure place in my personal pantheon (and they could be joined by a dozen more). I read and re-read them constantly. Their use of language, their gift of assembling "the right words in their best order" - as Coleridge defined poetry - is exemplary. I don't travel anywhere without a book (or three) of poetry in my bag. I've chosen poems that reflect the nocturnal theme of this little anthology but the hope lurking behind the exercise is that if you like this one poem by this particular poet then you will go and look for more. Think of each poem as a toothsome *hors d'oeuvre*, prelude to a magnificent banquet that awaits. Sweet dreams!

William Boyd

from 'Out on the lawn I lie in bed'

Out on the lawn I lie in bed,
Vega conspicuous overhead
  In the windless nights of June;
Forests of green have done complete
The day's activity; my feet
  Point to the rising moon.

Lucky, this point in time and space
Is chosen as my working place;
  Where the sexy airs of summer,
The bathing hours and the bare arms,
The leisured drives through a land of farms,
  Are good to the newcomer.

Equal with colleagues in a ring
I sit on each calm evening,
  Enchanted as the flowers
The opening light draws out of hiding
From leaves with all its dove-like pleading
  Its logic and its powers.

That later we, though parted then
May still recall these evenings when
  Fear gave his watch no look;
The lion griefs loped from the shade
And on our knees their muzzles laid,
  And Death put down his book.

W. H. Auden (1907 – 1973)

- 5 -

The Armadillo

This is the time of year
when almost every night
the frail, illegal fire balloons appear.
Climbing the mountain height,

rising toward a saint
still honored in these parts,
the paper chambers flush and fill with light
that comes and goes, like hearts.

Once up against the sky it's hard
to tell them from the stars –
planets, that is – the tinted ones:
Venus going down, or Mars,

or the pale green one. With a wind,
they flare and falter, wobble and toss;
but if it's still they steer between
the kite sticks of the Southern Cross,

receding, dwindling, solemnly
and steadily forsaking us,
or, in the downdraft from a peak,
suddenly turning dangerous.

Last night another big one fell.
It splattered like an egg of fire
against the cliff behind the house.
The flame ran down. We saw the pair

of owls who nest there flying up
and up, their whirling black-and-white
stained bright pink underneath, until
they shrieked up out of sight.

The ancient owls' nest must have burned.
Hastily, all alone,
a glistening armadillo left the scene,
rose-flecked, head down, tail down,

and then a baby rabbit jumped out,
short-eared, to our surprise.
So soft! – a handful of intangible ash
with fixed, ignited eyes.

Too pretty, dreamlike mimicry!
O falling fire and piercing cry
and panic, and a weak mailed fist
clenched ignorant against the sky!

Elizabeth Bishop (1911 – 1979)

Sad Steps

Groping back to bed after a piss
I part thick curtains, and am startled by
The rapid clouds, the moon's cleanliness.

Four o'clock: wedge-shadowed gardens lie
Under a cavernous, a wind-picked sky.
There's something laughable about this,

The way the moon dashes through clouds that blow
Loosely as cannon-smoke to stand apart
(Stone-coloured light sharpening the roofs below)

High and preposterous and separate –
Lozenge of love! Medallion of art!
O wolves of memory! Immensements! No,

One shivers slightly, looking up there.
The hardness and the brightness and the plain
Far-reaching singleness of that wide stare

Is a reminder of the strength and pain
Of being young; that it can't come again,
But is for others undiminished somewhere.

Philip Larkin (1922 – 1985)

from **Preludes**

I

The winter evening settles down
With smell of steaks in passageways.
Six o'clock.
The burnt-out ends of smoky days.
And now a gusty shower wraps
The grimy scraps
Of withered leaves about your feet
And newspapers from vacant lots;
The showers beat
On broken blinds and chimney-pots,
And at the corner of the street
A lonely cab-horse steams and stamps.

And then the lighting of the lamps.

T. S. Eliot (1888 – 1965)

Evening

Astounding lights
that the murk and poison
the breath of London produce

water-ice pinks or greens
a tingling haze
at once grimy and luscious

festive tatters
of cirrus perhaps
snagged at the edge

shot bonfire orange
as the yolk of the sun
blops into the west

the whole production
rigged up
just to pique your eye for a minute

through smeared glass
as it might be
upstairs on the slow bus home

what to do with it all
except get out your paintbox
Mr James Mallord William Turner

and slap it down
as best you can
in the damnable absence of elbow room

Christopher Reid

Champagne

The soulless matchmaking of lunar moths,
Uncanny, delicate or helpful, dove-coloured
Bosoms in the night: their fictions hurt us
Gently, like the nudity of rose-beige tea-gowns...

The mayflies' opera is their only moon, only
Those that fall on water reproduce, content
With scattering in fog or storm, such ivory
As elephants hold lofty, like champagne.

Medbh McGuckian

'Songs of Praise'

Tonight, their simple church grown glamorous,
The proud parishioners of the outlying parts
Lift up their hymn-books and their hearts
To please the outside-broadcast cameras.
The darkness deepens; day draws to a close;
A well-bred sixth-former yawns with her nose.

Outside, the hymn dies among rocks and dunes.
Conflicting rhythms of the incurious sea,
Not even contemptuous of these tiny tunes,
Take over where our thin ascriptions fail.
Down there the silence of the laboratory,
Trombone dispatches of the beleaguered whale.

Derek Mahon

Two Figures in Dense Violet Night

I had as lief be embraced by the porter at the hotel
As to get no more from the moonlight
Than your moist hand.

Be the voice of night and Florida in my ear.
Use dusky words and dusky images.
Darken your speech.

Speak, even, as if I did not hear you speaking,
But spoke for you perfectly in my thoughts,
Conceiving words,

As the night conceives the sea-sounds in silence,
And out of their droning sibilants makes
A serenade.

Say, puerile, that the buzzards crouch on the ridge-pole
And sleep with one eye watching the stars fall
Below Key West.

Say that the palms are clear in a total blue,
Are clear and are obscure; that it is night;
That the moon shines.

Wallace Stevens (1879 – 1955)

A Safe Distance

If the moon were closer, quite apart
from disasters it would wreak on earth,
how soon before that chiaroscuro,
the light-splashed pores and shadowy pits,
engrossing so much of the night sky
and dimming half the constellations,
would start to pall? By the same rule
the distance that divides us seems
providentially assigned so that
from here you still look radiant, majestic.

Jamie McKendrick

Heaven on Earth

Now that it is night,
you fetch in the washing
from outer space,

from the frozen garden
filmed like a kidney,
with a ghost in your mouth,

and everything you hold,
two floating shirts, a sheet,
ignores the law of gravity.

Only this morning,
the wren at her millinery,
making a baby's soft bonnet,

as we stopped by the spring,
watching the water
well up in the grass,

as if the world were teething.
It was heaven on earth
and it was only the morning.

Craig Raine

William Boyd is the author of three collections of short stories and twelve novels, the most recent of which are *Waiting for Sunrise* and *Solo*.